KING OF LIMBO

Act Now Plays

Series editor: Peter Rowlands
Founding editor: Andrew Bethell

Roots, Rules and Tribulations   Andrew Bethell
Closed Circuit   Mike English
Faust and Furious   Anne Lee
Czechmate   Gerry Docherty and Bill Kinross
Spring Offensive   Ray Speakman and Derek Nicholls
Football Apprentices   David Holman
Gregory's Girl   Bill Forsyth
Vacuees   Bill Martin
Easy on the Relish   Andrew Bethell
Fans   Mike English
Three Minute Heroes   Leslie Stewart
Wednesday's Child   Tony Higgins
The Tree that Holds up the Sky   Paul King
The Fourth Year are Animals   Richard Tulloch
Fit for Heroes   Charlie Moritz
Do We Ever See Grace?   Noël Greig
Rainbow's Ending   Noël Greig
Kidsplay   John Lee
Terms of Engagement   Martin Dimery
Hard to Swallow   Mark Wheeller
A Valuable Learning Experience   Gillian Wadds
Heroin Lies   Wayne Denfhy
Wolf Boy   Peter Charlton
Dags   Debra Oswald
A Nice Little Earner   Arnold Evans
Clean Up Your Act   Mike English
King of Limbo   Adrian Flynn

KING OF LIMBO
Adrian Flynn

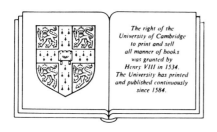

Cambridge University Press
CAMBRIDGE
NEW YORK   PORT CHESTER   MELBOURNE   SYDNEY

Published by the Press Syndicate of the University of Cambridge
The Pitt Building, Trumpington Street, Cambridge CB2 1RP
40 West 20th Street, New York, NY 10011, USA
10 Stamford Road, Oakleigh, Melbourne 3166, Australia

© Cambridge University Press 1991

First published 1991

Printed in Great Britain by
GreenShires Print Ltd, Kettering, Northamptonshire

British Library cataloguing in publication data

Flynn, Adrian 1956–
King of limbo – (Act now)
I. Title II. Series
822.914

ISBN 0 521 38752 3

GR

Performance
For permission to give a public performance of *King of Limbo* please write to Permissions Department, Cambridge University Press, The Edinburgh Building, Shaftesbury Road, Cambridge CB2 2RU.

Cover photograph by Aedan Kelly.

CHARACTERS

SAM FURNISS — A lively teenage boy who dreams of being a rock star. He becomes Kirk Klein in Rock 'n' Roll Limbo.

At school

DARRYL TAIT — A friend of Sam's. Pleasant but rather crafty.

LISA — Another friend. Always looking for a good laugh.

KAREN — Inseparable from Lisa. Full of life.

MR JACKSON — A firm but friendly teacher, used to dealing with teenagers.

At home

MR FURNISS — A miner. He's had a hard life and doesn't get much enjoyment out of it now. He doesn't understand his son any more.

MRS FURNISS — A kindly but long-suffering wife and mother. Determined to keep the family together.

Rock 'n' Roll Limbo

STIG — A good-natured punk rocker.

VINCE HOWELL — A ruthless businessman, who doesn't care who he hurts.

JENNY — A goth. A thoughtful and hard-headed character.

GENE — A rock and roller who models himself on Elvis Presley.

ZETA — The wild and eccentric head of the Ever-ready Church.

RAEL, STEEL, JOOLZ — Three streetwise reporters, keen to get the facts fast.

THE DANCER — A snakey, menacing character. Quite bitter and cruel.

THE EVER-READIES   Zeta's energetic followers.

Extras

Rock and roll dancers to accompany Gene.
Half-human, half-reptile acolytes for The Dancer.
TV camera crews, radio crews and rock fans.

A NOTE ON PRODUCTION

The play does not need any complicated scenery to make it work. Where things are needed, like chairs for the Furniss's living room, they can be taken on and off by the actors themselves.

If possible, one area of the acting space should be higher than the rest, to act as Sam's bedroom, Zeta's pulpit and the concert stage. This could be achieved quite simply by the use of stage blocks.

Where stage lighting is available, blackouts can be used as an effective way to change some scenes, particularly when the action moves from earth to Rock 'n' Roll Limbo and back again. An imaginative use of coloured lights may add a great deal to the atmosphere of Limbo. How much music and dance is used during the play depends very much on the strengths of the particular cast performing it. The only essential dance is the one The Dancer performs, but there are opportunities for dances in the Church of the Ever-readies, in Gene's scene and in other places for that matter.

Costumes and make-up are important in making *King of Limbo* entertaining to watch. There is a great deal of opportunity for imitating or creating rock styles. Every character in Rock 'n' Roll Limbo should have their own definite, fantastic look. Your imagination is the only limit on this.

Finally, a p.a. system with a microphone offstage for The Dancer's first speeches and to play music through would be very useful, though not essential.

Good luck!

STAGE DIRECTIONS

There are two kinds of directions in this playscript. Those in **bold type** provide information that is essential to an understanding of what is happening in the play at the time. For a play-reading, these should be read by a separate reader.

Those in *italic type* are less essential stage directions and offer suggestions to assist with a production of the play onstage. In a reading they are best not read out as they will hamper the flow of the play, although those who are reading may find that some of these instructions offer help with the interpretation of their lines.

A SCHOOL PLAYGROUND. LATE AFTERNOON

(LISA is painting her nails. KAREN is chewing gum. DARRYL is listening to some music from a huge cassette recorder. They all look bored. Darryl, in a world of his own, starts dancing to the music. He is enthusiastic, rather than talented. Karen stares at him amazed, then nudges LISA to look as well. They burst out laughing. Darryl stops, embarrassed, and switches off the tape. Lisa and Karen tap their heads as though he's an idiot.)

DARRYL   Well, I'm bored.

LISA   Me too.

KAREN   How long's Jackson gonna keep him in there?

A CLASSROOM

(SAM is being spoken to by MR JACKSON.)

MR JACKSON   What did you think you were up to, Sam?

SAM   What do you mean, sir?

MR JACKSON   You know very well what I mean. I left the classroom for a moment and when I got back you were leaping around on your desk and shrieking like a scalded cat.

SAM   Oh, that?

MR JACKSON   Yes, that.

SAM   I was only doing what you said, sir.

MR JACKSON   I didn't say anything of the sort.

SAM   You did, sir. Before you left the room, you asked us to be thinking about our future.

MR JACKSON   Well?

SAM	That is my future, sir.
MR JACKSON	Jumping around like an electrified frog?
SAM	No, sir. I'm going to be a rock superstar.
MR JACKSON	*(Understanding)* Oh . . .
SAM	With millions of adoring fans at my concerts. Like Michael Jackson.
MR JACKSON	I see.
SAM	I was practising being mobbed when you came back in.
MR JACKSON	I never knew you were a good singer.
SAM	Oh yeah . . . well, no, not actually, sir.
MR JACKSON	Well, what instrument do you play?
SAM	I don't play any instrument, sir.
MR JACKSON	So you can't read or write music?
SAM	I don't need to. I'm not trying to be Beethoven, sir. I want to be a rock star.
MR JACKSON	There's a lot of hard work goes into being a good pop musician, you know, Sam.
SAM	It's your personality that counts, sir. And I've got bags of that.
MR JACKSON	So have thousands of kids your age. You're not all going to become 'superstars', are you? Be realistic.
SAM	I am being realistic. It's what I really want to do.
MR JACKSON	Why?
SAM	That's obvious, isn't it, sir?
MR JACKSON	The money?
SAM	No not really . . . People look up to you, don't they? You're different. You're special.
MR JACKSON	And that's important?
SAM	Of course it is, sir. I want to do something with my life. I don't want to end up like my dad.

MR JACKSON	He works at the colliery doesn't he?
SAM	Yeah, and he hates it. He comes home every night completely knackered . . . sorry, sir . . . and he just slumps in front of the telly like a zombie. That's it. Work, TV and twice a week down the boozer till he can't stand up. No one's got any respect for him. Not even himself. I'm not going to be like that.
MR JACKSON	No one says you have to be.
SAM	It's what you mean by being realistic though, isn't it, sir? Don't think too big. Don't get above yourself.
MR JACKSON	Look, Sam. If you're serious about being a musician, have you thought of arranging lessons here? You could learn to play the guitar after school.
SAM	I get lessons all day, sir. I'm up to here with them. I don't want any more.
MR JACKSON	It was just a thought.
SAM	Can I go now, sir? You've kept me ages.
MR JACKSON	Yes, Sam. As long as you promise not to fool around like that again.
SAM	*(Angelic)* No, sir.
MR JACKSON	And think about what I said.
SAM	Oh yes, sir. Thank you, sir.

THE PLAYGROUND

(SAM **joins his friends.**)

DARRYL	Where've you been?
LISA	We were going to send out search parties.
SAM	Mr Jackson was being sympathetic.
KAREN	Oh that takes ages.
DARRYL	I wish they'd just give you lines and let you get off.

KAREN   What did he say?

SAM   That I've got to have lessons if I want to be a superstar.

DARRYL   What?

LISA   Does he think Madonna had to be taught how to be Madonna?

KAREN   Teachers have no idea, have they?

SAM   When I make the big time, I'm going to come back here in a stretch limousine . . . a fantastic-looking woman on each arm . . .

(LISA **and** KAREN **take hold of his arms. He brushes them off.**)

Not you two! . . . and I'll offer Jackson the chance to be one of my roadies.

DARRYL   What's one of them?

SAM   They lug all your gear round for you. Set things up.

DARRYL   Jackson wouldn't do that.

SAM   He will if I offer him ten thousand a week. You can get anyone to do anything if you've got enough money.

DARRYL   Hey, can I be a ropey?

SAM   Roadie!

DARRYL   I'd do it for five thousand a week.

SAM   You can't even change a light-bulb safely.

DARRYL   I'll sell you me brother's guitar cheap if you'll let me.

SAM   What?

KAREN   Does Terry know you're selling it?

DARRYL   He asked me to. It's no use to him now he's in the army.

SAM   How much?

DARRYL   I'm meant to ask for a hundred, but I'll let you have it for seventy.

SAM   Seventy quid!

DARRYL   It's got its own amplifier.
LISA   That's a bargain, Sam. You should take it.
KAREN   You could use it at the talent night at the Youthie.
LISA   Next Tuesday.
KAREN   You could mime to a record or something.
LISA   It would impress Tracy Phillips.
SAM   Who says I want to impress her?
LISA   I bet you'd look dead good with a guitar.
DARRYL   It's black and silver. Really flash.
KAREN   It'd look great with your black shirt and jeans. *(Slight pause)*
SAM   My parents would never lend me the money.
LISA   That's Sam all over, isn't it?
KAREN   All mouth.
LISA   You'll never be a rock star.
KAREN   'Mummy won't give me the money.'
SAM   All right! I will get it. I'll show you. And I'll show Jackson too. You just bring it down to the Youthie tonight, Darryl.
DARRYL   Are you really going to buy it?
SAM   Yeah.
DARRYL   Where're you going to get the money?
SAM   Never you mind. Just bring it, all right?
DARRYL   Right.
SAM   See you later then.
DARRYL   Yeah.
SAM   And don't forget the guitar.
LISA /
KAREN   } See ya!

SAM'S HOUSE. THE LIVING ROOM

(SAM **and his parents,** MR **and** MRS FURNISS, **are sitting in front of the TV. Mrs Furniss is knitting. Mr Furniss is engrossed in the programme. Sam is getting restless.**)

SAM Dad . . .

MR FURNISS Sssh, son. Not now.

SAM But it's important.

MR FURNISS Can't you see I'm watching this? It'll have to wait.

SAM *(Sighs)* Mum . . .

MRS FURNISS Not now love . . . not while your dad's programme's on. (SAM **puts on his personal stereo and switches it on. He is listening to something fast and angry. He punches the air in time with the music. The TV programme ends.**)

MR FURNISS That was very good. You could learn a lot from the television Sam. (**He turns to look at Sam.**) What's the matter with him? Is he having some kind of fit?

(MRS FURNISS **taps** SAM's **arm and mouths 'Turn it off.' Sam does so and takes off the earphones.**)

MR FURNISS *(Standing up)* I've a good mind to take that off you.

SAM Why?

MR FURNISS You put those things on and you're off into a world of your own. It's not healthy.

SAM *(About to argue, then swallows it)* Dad, can I ask a favour?

MR FURNISS *(Leaving room)* Not now, Sam. I'll be late for darts. Ask me later.

(**He exits.**)

SAM It's always later!

MRS FURNISS Can't you ask me, love?

SAM I want to borrow some money.

MRS FURNISS Hm . . .

SAM	It's important.
MRS FURNISS	I might have a bit of change in my purse.
SAM	I need seventy quid.
MRS FURNISS	Pardon?
SAM	Terry Tait's selling a guitar.
MRS FURNISS	Seventy pounds?
SAM	It's a bargain.
MRS FURNISS	Where's that sort of money coming from?
SAM	I'll pay it back out of me Saturday job.
MRS FURNISS	By the time you've paid us back, you'll have lost all interest in it.
SAM	I won't. It's what I really want.
MRS FURNISS	That's what you said about American Football, remember?
SAM	I was only a kid then.
MRS FURNISS	We bought all that stuff and you hardly touched it. It's just lying idle in your cupboard now, isn't it?
SAM	But I'm serious about this. Really serious. *(Mrs Furniss looks at him for a moment.)* Please.

(MR FURNISS **comes back in, putting on a jacket.**)

MR FURNISS	I'm off now.
MRS FURNISS	Derek, what would you think of Sam buying a guitar?
MR FURNISS	Not a lot.
MRS FURNISS	He's got the chance of one cheap.
MR FURNISS	I don't care if it comes free in his cornflakes. He wastes too much time on pop music as it is.
SAM	Dad, it's what I really want. More than anything.
MR FURNISS	You're not having it.
SAM	Please.
MR FURNISS	Over my dead body.

SAM	*(Gets up and storms out)* Thanks for nothing!
MR FURNISS	Hey! Come back here! *(Door slams offstage.)* Right. I'll sort him out when I get back this evening.
MRS FURNISS	Don't be too hard on him, Derek.
MR FURNISS	He thinks too much of his blessed music, that lad. It's changed him. And not for the better.

THE YOUTH CLUB

(KAREN **and** LISA **are sitting looking bored. Karen is holding a canned drink. In the background there is some pop music.** DARRYL **enters, carrying the guitar and amp.**)

LISA	*(Jumping up)* Hey, brilliant! Let's have a go.
DARRYL	Careful!

(LISA **snatches the guitar from him.** KAREN **stands up and looks at it.**)

KAREN	Doesn't it look great?

(**She starts tunelessly singing any current pop song, using the can as a microphone.** LISA **joins in, miming being an over-the-top rock guitarist.**)

DARRYL	Come on, sit down. Everyone in Youthie's looking at us.
KAREN	That's what I want. *(Lisa and Karen laugh.)*
LISA	This guitar's brilliant. I want one.
KAREN	*(Pointing to the amp)* Don't think much of that though. It's held together with sticky tape. There's wires sticking out all over.
LISA	What's it matter? No one looks at that . . . Hiya, Sam! *(Sam enters.)*
DARRYL	I've brought it. Have you got the money?

(LISA **gives** SAM **the guitar.**)

SAM	It's beautiful.

DARRYL	Have you got the cash with you?
KAREN	Are you going to buy it, Sam?
SAM	I can't. They wouldn't give me the money.
LISA	*(To Karen)* Told you so.
DARRYL	You don't have to pay straightaway. My brother won't be on leave for another three months.
SAM	Honest?
DARRYL	Yeah.
SAM	I could easily save seventy pounds in three months.
DARRYL	Take it then.
SAM	You're sure?
DARRYL	Yeah.
SAM	Thanks. I will pay you, honest . . . Can I take it?
DARRYL	Yeah.

(SAM **picks up the amp as well and starts to leave.**)

KAREN	Are you going?
SAM	I can't wait to get started. I want to be ready for talent night. Thanks Darryl. See you. *(He exits.)*
LISA	You're trusting.
DARRYL	I was glad to get it off me hands, to be honest. Everyone else who's looked at it said it was rubbish.

SAM'S HOUSE. SAM'S BEDROOM

(SAM **is standing with the guitar, acknowledging a crowd of imaginary fans.**)

SAM	Thank you, thank you so much. We're going to play one more number before we go . . .

MRS FURNISS	*(Offstage)* Sam . . . Sam! Is that you? *(She enters.)* I didn't hear you come in . . . What's that doing here?
SAM	Darryl said I could pay over three months.
MRS FURNISS	Your dad said you couldn't have it.
SAM	Well, I've got it now.
MRS FURNISS	How dare you! . . . He'll throw it out.
SAM	He won't!
MRS FURNISS	Sam, you've no right to be disobedient in this house.
SAM	And you've no right to stop me being what I want to be.
MRS FURNISS	He's mad enough with you as it is. He'll go crazy when he sees this.
SAM	He's always going crazy.
MRS FURNISS	Stop being stupid.
SAM	I'm not being stupid.
MRS FURNISS	He'll throw you out.
SAM	Let him.

(Pause. MRS FURNISS and SAM stand looking at each other.)

MRS FURNISS	God help us. I don't understand my own family any more.

(She exits. SAM connects the guitar to the amp and adjusts a control. There is a flash and he falls to the floor. From offstage, we hear MRS FURNISS.)

MRS FURNISS	Sam, what's happened? Are you all right? *(She enters and hurries over to Sam.)* Sam! Sam! Sam! . . . Sam! Sam!

(The lights fade to blackout. In the dark we hear a crowd shouting 'Soul-saver! Soul-saver!')

THE OFFICE OF VINCE HOWELL

(The shouts fade away as the lights come back up to reveal a few chairs, but no other furniture. STIG is putting a sign up in the room 'Welcome to the Soul-saver, Kirk Klein'. VINCE HOWELL enters.)

VINCE	Aren't you done, yet?
STIG	Almost, Mr Howell.
VINCE	He'll be here any minute . . . We want to create the right impression. This is going to be the biggest day ever in Rock 'n' Roll Limbo, Stig.
STIG	I know, Mr Howell.
VINCE	*(Taking hold of Stig by collar)* So I don't want anyone messing it up. Understand?
STIG	No, Mr Howell. Yes, Mr Howell.
VINCE	*(Lets go of Stig)* You've made all the arrangements?
STIG	The TV, radio and press are all coming here as soon as the Soul-saver arrives.
VINCE	Good. We've got to put him in the mood for tonight's concert.
STIG	I can't wait. We're all going to be set free.
VINCE	Thanks to me! Vince Howell. Mr Big in Limbo. And I'm going to be Mr Big in Rock 'n' Roll Heaven.
STIG	You're the greatest . . .
VINCE	Shut up Stig . . . I *am* the greatest, because I've found the Soul-saver. No one else could.
STIG	Only Vince Howell.
VINCE	Shut up Stig . . . Only Vince Howell could find the one they were all looking for. And people had better be grateful.
STIG	They will be, Mr Howell . . .
VINCE	Shut up, Stig . . . I hear something.

(Crowd noise offstage, like fans around rock star)

STIG	It must be the Soul-saver.
VINCE	It is; I can see Jenny with him.
STIG	*(Very excited)* Wow! The Soul-saver! Yeeeeaaah!
VINCE	Stig . . .

STIG   I know. Shut up.

(SAM, **now in a rock star costume, stumbles onstage.** JENNY **follows, trying to hold back the crowd that wants to follow on.**)

JENNY   Back off now. You'll see Kirk at the concert.

VINCE   *(Approaching Sam)* Kirk baby.

(**He shakes** SAM's **hand vigorously, then goes up to crowd.**)

Go away now, or there'll be no concert tonight . . . The Soul-saver wants some peace and quiet.

(**Crowd noise dies away and the crowd disappears.**)

STIG   Mr Klein, it'd be an honour to shake your hand.

SAM   Thanks very much, but I'm not Mr Klein.

STIG   Who are you?

SAM   I'm . . . er . . .

VINCE   You're Kirk Klein now, kid. The Soul-saver.

SAM   I had another name . . . I can't remember it.

VINCE   That happens to everyone when they get here. Just get used to your new name. You're going to hear it a lot.

SAM   Kirk?

JENNY   Kirk Klein.

SAM   Kirk Klein.

VINCE   That's it, kid.

JENNY   Mr Howell, I think the media have arrived.

VINCE   Come and sit down, Kirk baby. We've got a quick press conference to deal with . . . Let 'em in, Jenny.

JENNY   *(Ushering on reporters, photographers, camera crews)* This way, please.

VINCE   OK, ladies and gentlemen. You'll appreciate Kirk is tired after his long journey, so let's keep this short and sweet.

JOOLZ   Are you looking forward to the concert tonight, Kirk?

SAM	Er... who's playing? *(Reporters laugh.)*
RAEL	Why are you so keen to play?
SAM	Well...
JOOLZ	Is it because it's such a special gig?
SAM	Erm...
STEEL	Are you really sure you're the Soul-saver?
SAM	Am I sure I'm what?
STEEL	The Soul-saver.
JOOLZ	The star who's going to open the gates of Rock 'n' Roll Limbo?
RAEL	The mega-star superstar?
SAM	Ah...
JOOLZ	Are you...
STEEL	really...
RAEL	sure?
VINCE	Of course he is. Aren't you, kid?

(Pause. Everyone is waiting expectantly on SAM's answer.)

SAM	Er... yes.

(Everyone cheers and applauds.)

VINCE	That's it, ladies and gentlemen. Kirk's going off to his hotel to relax before tonight's concert. I hope you'll respect his privacy.
RAEL	*(Leaving)* Thanks, Kirk.
STEEL	Good luck.
JOOLZ	We're all depending on you.

(Reporters and rest of media exit.)

VINCE	Well done, kid. You handled it like a professional.
SAM	Oh good. By the way...
VINCE	Yeah?

SAM	What exactly does a Soul-saver do?
VINCE	The journey has shaken you up, Kirk baby.
STIG	You've just got to be yourself.
JENNY	Play great rock and roll guitar at the concert tonight.
VINCE	And you'll open the gates of this prison.
SAM	And you're sure I'm going to do that?
VINCE	Of course we're sure, kid. I've never seen anyone in such a hurry to get here from Earth.
JENNY	That's how we know.
STIG	Anyway, you said you were the Soul-saver just now.
SAM	Right.
VINCE	*(Threatening)* You were telling the truth there, Kirk?
SAM	Oh yes.
VINCE	Great. Take him to the hotel then, Jenny. And Kirk?
SAM	Yeah?
VINCE	Thanks for coming to save us. You've made this a great day in Limbo.

(JENNY, SAM, STIG and VINCE exit. Blackout.)

THE CHURCH OF THE EVER-READIES

(Lights up. The congregation enter dancing to some rock music. ZETA goes onto the stage blocks to address them when all are present.)

ZETA	Brothers and sisters, we are gathered again; the faithful, the ever-willing, the always prepared, Church of the Ever-readies. We are the Ever-readies.
CONGREGATION	The Ever-readies!
ZETA	A battery of believers, making the current flow in Limbo. Let's flow brothers and sisters.

	(The congregation pass an electric current back and forth in breakdance fashion.)
	You may be seated, brethren.
	(The congregation sit down.)
	Today is a great day for all us bright sparks. You will have seen on your TV screens that we're finally going to be discharged.
ONE MEMBER OF CONGREGATION	*(Jumping up)* Hallelujah!
ZETA	*(Gives withering look)* Today we're going to make that big jump between terminals. Kirk Klein, the Soul-saver, is going to throw the switch that sends us surging through the ether. There'll be no resistance. We're not going to be ampered; we're finally going ohm.
SAME MEMBER OF CONGREGATION	Ohm, sweet ohm.
ZETA	*(Another withering look)* So let's switch onto standby for a while to recharge. This is Zeta Morita, your electric preacher telling all you live-wires to be here again this afternoon, when we'll plug back into the cosmic mains.
CONGREGATION	Socket to us!
	(ZETA and the congregation dance out over something like 'Electric Dreams', by Giorgio Moroder and Phil Oakey. Lights down.)

THE HOTEL ROOM

	(Lights go up on a smart guitar and amp. SAM and JENNY are on.)
SAM	Wow! What a fantastic hotel room.

JENNY Nothing but the best will do.

SAM A king-size water-bed . . . a cocktail cabinet . . . my own bathroom suite . . . with a gold-plated toilet-roll holder!

JENNY It's the star suite.

SAM It's too good for me.

JENNY Nothing's too good for the Soul-saver.

SAM I hope I'm going to be worth it.

JENNY You will be.

SAM Maybe I'd better have a little practice before tonight.

JENNY You see. None of the others bothered to practise.

SAM What others?

JENNY There've been plenty. People claiming to be the Soul-saver.

SAM What happened to them?

JENNY Most of them chickened out before the concert. Some of them tried to bluff their way out – went ahead and played. Boy, were they awful. *(Laughs)*

SAM Where are they now?

JENNY Still here. Waiting for you to get us out.

(SAM **picks up the guitar. He shapes to play it, then puts it down.**)

I'll let you practise alone.

SAM Thanks.

JENNY I'll be right next door if you want me.

(JENNY **exits.** SAM **picks up the guitar again. He is in two minds about trying to play it. Finally he tries a couple of chords. They sound awful.**)

SAM I can't play... They think I'm a superstar and I still can't play the guitar.

(He looks out to an imaginary audience.)

Thank you, thank you. Hey, you know when I said I was going to save you all with my guitar-playing? I was just kidding. Good joke, eh?

(He recoils from hostile response.)

They'll kill me.

(He steps forward and addresses imaginary audience again.)

Thank you, thank you very much. Hey, I've got some news for you. I broke both my arms this afternoon, so I can't play tonight. We'll just have to hum the tunes together.

(To himself)

That's it. Break my fingers!

(He tries to think of a way to do this. He jams his hand in his mouth and tries to bite it. He gives up.)

Jenny! Jenny!

JENNY *(Entering)* What is it, chief?

SAM Get me a hammer.

JENNY Sure. What for?

SAM To break my fingers with.

JENNY OK. *(Starts to go out, then stops and double-takes.)* What?

SAM I'd like you to bash my hands with a hammer.

JENNY Why, are you crazy?

SAM It'll give me an excuse not to play tonight.

JENNY Why do you want an excuse?

SAM Because I can't play.

JENNY Oh Kirk... *(Puts arm round him)* Every star feels like that once in a while...

SAM   I can't play tonight!

JENNY   It's natural for you to be nervous . . .

SAM   It's not nerves.

JENNY   Of course it is.

SAM   It's the simple fact I don't know how to play guitar.

JENNY   *(Pause)* Kirk. Please. You're kidding?

SAM   I'm not.

JENNY   You don't know how to play guitar?

SAM   No.

JENNY   Then why have you come here as the Soul-saver?

SAM   It was a mistake. I didn't want to come.

JENNY   You were in an almighty rush to get here.

SAM   I don't remember.

JENNY   That's why we were so sure . . . and now we're still going to be stuck here!

SAM   Sorry.

JENNY   Why did you lie at the press conference?

SAM   I didn't.

JENNY   You did!

SAM   I thought . . .

JENNY   What?

SAM   That somehow I'd find I could play well.

JENNY   You fool!

SAM   It seemed so incredible. Everyone calling me the Soul-saver. I thought maybe I was.

JENNY   Everyone had faith in you.

SAM   I know.

JENNY   So what are you going to do?

SAM   I'll admit I was lying. I'll apologise.

JENNY The whole of Limbo was waiting to be saved. They'll hate you.
SAM Other people have tried to be Soul-savers.
JENNY None of them was as sure as you. And none of them was promoted by Vince Howell. When he finds out you were lying, this won't be Limbo for you; it'll be Hell.
SAM What can I do?
JENNY *(Slight pause)* There's nowhere to hide.
SAM I'll go out now and tell them.
JENNY Wait. What time is it?
SAM Six.
JENNY You don't have to be at the stadium till 9. You've got one slight chance.
SAM What?
JENNY We're going to see Gene. *(Starts to exit)*
SAM Who?
JENNY Gene. Come on.

(Blackout. Lights up on a group rock 'n' roll number in the style of Elvis Presley or Gene Vincent. When the number ends, rock 'n' roll dancers go off, leaving GENE centre-stage. He takes a bread roll from his pocket, which he uses as a microphone as he gyrates alone on stage.)

GENE Huh,
Uh, huh huh,
Hey yeah,
Uh, huh huh. *(Repeat)*

(He is about to bite the roll when JENNY and SAM enter.)

JENNY Gene!
GENE Jenny, baby. Who's the dude?
JENNY This is Kirk.
GENE Kirk Klein! Fantastic.

(He goes to shake SAM's hand, remembering to transfer the roll at the last moment. Sam then has to wipe his hand on his trousers.)

It's an honour to meet you.

JENNY	No it's not.
GENE	Jenny, are you crazy? He's the Soul-saver.
JENNY	No he's not.
GENE	He is! Now I recognise him from TV. You were on TV earlier, weren't you, Kirk?
SAM	Yes...
JENNY	He's a fraud. He's admitted it.
GENE	You're not going to play good enough to get us out of here?
SAM	Sorry.
GENE	Oh no. I was so sure... Does Vince Howell know yet?
JENNY	Not yet.
GENE	He'll tear this boy apart, piece by piece.
JENNY	The crowd'll do that.
GENE	The crowd won't stand a chance against Vince; he's an animal when he's mad and he's gonna be so mad about this, he'll destroy the kid.
SAM	Thanks. You're really cheering me up.
JENNY	You're the only person who could help us, Gene.
GENE	How? This kid's a turkey. A total goofball. He's beyond help.
SAM	I don't have to take this.
JENNY	You'll take this and more. You've got into this mess; now you've got to find a way out.
GENE	How? There's no way out for him.
JENNY	You remember your concert, Gene? We thought you might save us all.
GENE	I don't like to think about it.
JENNY	You were good.
GENE	Not good enough.

JENNY	The best we've ever had here.
GENE	Well?
JENNY	Teach Kirk a few of your moves and a couple of songs.
GENE	*(Laughing)* What good'll that do?
SAM	I won't learn enough in an hour or two …
GENE	Remember, I couldn't do it good enough after practising all my life.
JENNY	I know he won't be good. But if he does *something*, people won't be so angry. Vince might not get so mad at him.
GENE	He won't be any good.
JENNY	At least he'll have tried.
GENE	I don't know.
JENNY	Please.
GENE	Kid?
SAM	I've got nothing to lose. It might help.
JENNY	And he's going to have to live here for a very long time.
GENE	OK. Come here, kid. Follow me.

(GENE **faces straight out, takes up Elvis posture, sneer on lips.** SAM **tries to copy.**)

SAM	*(Through twisted lips)* Like this?
GENE	It'll have to do. Now try this.

Uh huh huh,
Uh huh huh,
Hey yeah.

SAM	Ah hah hah, Ah hah hah, Hey yah.
GENE	Hold it! This isn't an elocution lesson. You've got to mumble it a little. Curl your lip some more.
SAM	Like this?

GENE Sort of. Now try again.

Uh huh huh.

SAM *(Complete mumble)* Mmm, mmmuh, mmmuh.

GENE Forget the singing for a moment, Kirk. Let's see if we can get a few moves right.

SAM OK.

GENE Let's jus' loosen up a little.

(He goes through some Elvis-type gyrations.)

Now you.

(SAM makes some very stiff and jerky movements.)

Give me strength.

JENNY Be patient with him, Gene.

GENE Try and be looser, kid. Like this.

(He gyrates and does a couple of kicks. SAM tries the same and falls over.)

SAM How'm I doing?

GENE I've seen more talent in a dead sheep. You know what I'd do in your shoes, Kirk?

SAM What?

GENE When you first go onstage, tell the punters you're a complete fraud . . .

JENNY Gene!

GENE They might beat you up a little but it'll be ten times worse if they see you perform.

SAM Am I that bad?

GENE Kid, you're not bad. You're baaaad! And when I say baaaad, I do not mean good.

JENNY Don't be so hard on him.

GENE There's no point letting him fool himself.

SAM So what can I do?

JENNY	Good question. Any bright ideas?
GENE	*(Slight pause)* Well . . . you could see Zeta.
JENNY	Not Zeta.
SAM	Who or what is Zeta?
JENNY	You know the Catholics have a pope on earth?
SAM	Yeah.
JENNY	Well, Zeta is sort of the pope here. She's the head of the Ever-readies.
SAM	The who?
JENNY	The Ever-readies. Sort of religious freaks.
GENE	Boy, are they freaks!
JENNY	They're the ones who believe most in a Soul-saver.
SAM	Won't she be the angriest of the lot when she finds out I'm a fake?
JENNY	Yeah. It's not a good idea.
GENE	Listen. She said something to me once . . .
JENNY	What?
GENE	After my concert, she came up to me. She sort of hinted that she knew something that could have made it work, that could have saved us.
SAM	What was it?
GENE	She wouldn't say. It was too late, after the concert. But I think she knows something other people don't.
SAM	Let's go and see her.
JENNY	She's quite a strange lady.
SAM	She might be my only help. Thanks, Gene. Come on. Which way do we go?
	(He exits. JENNY starts to follow.)
JENNY	Yeah thanks. Are you going to go tonight?

GENE: I don't think so. I don't much like the sight of blood. Good luck.

(JENNY exits. GENE takes his bread roll out again and starts to do an Elvis-type dance as the lights dim to blackout.)

THE CHURCH OF THE EVER-READIES

(Lights up on dance number. ZETA enters pulpit.)

ZETA: Brothers and sisters, I have a message of hope for you all, because today you are being given a gift.

CONGREGATION: A gift!

ZETA: You are being given your freedom by the Soul-saver.

CONGREGATION: The Soul-saver!

ZETA: Your freedom is like a nut, from which the tree of happiness will grow. Kirk Klein, the Soul-saver, will give these nuts to you.

CONGREGATION: Nuts to you!

ZETA: Let us glow and grow, brethren...

(JENNY and SAM enter.)

CONGREGATION: Wow! The Soul-saver!

(The Ever-readies crowd excitedly round SAM.)

ZETA: Brothers and sisters! Show some dignity in the House of the Eternally Charged.

JENNY: Could we speak to you, Zeta? Alone?

ZETA: Brethren, you may discharge.

(Disappointed grumbles from crowd.)

Go on now, Ever-readies, don't be shocked.

(Crowd goes off. ZETA comes down from pulpit.)

You must forgive them. It's only natural they should get excited when they see the man who's going to save us all.

SAM	Er... yeah...
JENNY	That's what we've come to see you about.
ZETA	I'd be so honoured if I could help in any way.
JENNY	We're hoping you can.
ZETA	What can I do?
JENNY	Are you sure no one can hear us?
ZETA	There's no one else here.
JENNY	Go on, Kirk.
SAM	Well... er... it's like this... erm...
ZETA	I'm completely trustworthy, Soul-saver.
SAM	Suppose...
ZETA	Yes?
SAM	I wasn't really the Soul-saver?
ZETA	*(Laughs)* What a ridiculous idea. We all know you are. Aren't you?
JENNY	That's the problem.
ZETA	You're not the Soul-saver?
SAM	I'm not sure. Well, probably not, really...
JENNY	Definitely not. *(Zeta screams)* He can't even play the guitar, let alone save us.
ZETA	You said you were on the TV!
SAM	I know.
ZETA	We believed you.
SAM	Yes, I'm sorry.
ZETA	*(Very upset)* We were certain you were real.
JENNY	*(To Sam)* Now do you understand the harm you've done?
SAM	I've made a fool of myself.
ZETA	You've destroyed all our hopes.

SAM: I'm really sorry. I'd do anything to make it up.

ZETA: Hah! How can you put right a thousand shattered dreams?

SAM: I'd do anything.

ZETA: What could you do?

SAM: We thought you might know.

JENNY: A long time ago, you hinted to Gene that you knew something. How to make someone a Soul-saver.

ZETA: *(Horrified)* He should never have spoken of this!

SAM: What was the secret?

ZETA: Don't ask! I didn't know then what was involved.

SAM: Please tell me. I'd do anything.

JENNY: No, Kirk. It doesn't sound right.

SAM: Please tell me.

ZETA: *(Thoughtfully)* Yet . . . you've brought it on yourself, by the lie you told this morning.

JENNY: Zeta, we don't want any more trouble than we've already got.

ZETA: Yes. You owe it to us to take the risk.

JENNY: Come on, Kirk. Let's go.

SAM: I'm staying, Jenny.

ZETA: Good.

JENNY: *(Taking his arm)* Come on!

SAM: *(Gently releasing himself)* I'm staying. I'm going to make up for what I've done.

ZETA: If you stay, I must blindfold you.

JENNY: She's crazy.

SAM: I accept.

JENNY: Don't! It sounds too dangerous.

SAM: Leave me, Jenny. I've got to go through with it.

ZETA	*(Blindfolds Sam. To Jenny)* Go, while you still can!
	(JENNY exits. ZETA starts to lead SAM on a journey. This can be as short or long as the playing space, imagination of the two actors and technical resources allow. There should be some background electronic music and subtly changing lights as they move round the space. They stop centre-stage.)
ZETA	*(Calling)* Are you there? Are you there?
SAM	Who are you calling?
ZETA	Be silent! *(Calling)* Are you there?
THE DANCER	*(Offstage. Voice amplified)* You're here again?
ZETA	Yes.
THE DANCER	You remember what I told you last time?
ZETA	I've brought someone to keep my side of the bargain.
THE DANCER	Good. Let me see him.
	(ZETA **stands to one side.** THE DANCER **appears on the raised part of the stage. His acolytes appear onstage. There should be a snakey or reptilian quality about them all.**)
	Does he understand the bargain?
ZETA	He knows nothing yet.
THE DANCER	If he doesn't agree, your soul will be forfeit, Zeta.
ZETA	He will agree.
THE DANCER	Let him see me.
	(ZETA **removes the blindfold.**)
	What is your name?
SAM	Kirk Klein.
THE DANCER	Why are you here?
SAM	I want to be the Soul-saver.
THE DANCER	How?
SAM	By playing well tonight.

THE DANCER	No matter what the cost?
SAM	*(Slight pause)* I'll pay any price.
THE DANCER	Then watch.

(**THE DANCER performs a very lively, exotic dance with the acolytes. ZETA and SAM watch from the side.**)

THE DANCER	*(Having finished)* What did you think?
SAM	Brilliant.
THE DANCER	Do you want to know how I dance so well?
SAM	Yes.
THE DANCER	*(Beckons an acolyte over, who gives The Dancer a phial)* I dance like that, because I feed on the moonstone. *(Holding up the phial)* Do you see it? Isn't it beautiful?
SAM	What is it?
THE DANCER	It is the way of life. You must taste it if you are to be the Soul-saver.

(**SAM reaches for it. THE DANCER draws it away.**)

Ah! You don't know the price.

SAM	I'd pay anything. Only I don't have anything to pay with.
THE DANCER	Oh, but you have.
SAM	What?
THE DANCER	The rest of your life.
SAM	What do you mean?
THE DANCER	If you take the moonstone, you will play well enough to open the gates of Limbo. Everyone will leave, except you. You must stay.
SAM	How long for?
THE DANCER	For ever. You will never leave Limbo. It's the only place you will find the moonstone.
SAM	I won't need it, once I've played.

THE DANCER	Once you've tasted it, you will always need it. You will never be able to leave.
SAM	*(To Zeta)* Is this true?
ZETA	The Dancer knows of what he speaks.
SAM	*(To The Dancer)* How do you know?
THE DANCER	A long time ago, there were many more souls trapped here. I was one of them. By chance, I found the moonstone and discovered that, using it, I could dance like a genius. I danced so well I opened the gates of Limbo. Everyone left for the Rock 'n' Roll Heaven. Everyone but me. I couldn't drag myself away from the moonstone.
SAM	Could you open the gates again for all of us?
THE DANCER	Perhaps. But I won't. I want someone else to share what I suffer. Someone better than these wretches. *(He waves his arm at the acolytes, who cower)* . . . for eternal company. Someone else must take the moonstone.
SAM	Is it such a bad life here? I don't think I'd mind staying.
THE DANCER	Look child.

(**THE DANCER removes mask to reveal hideously distorted features.**)

This is what the moonstone does to you.

(**He holds out the phial.**)

Take it. *(Sam hesitates)* Take it! Your soul against all the souls in Limbo.

(**SAM takes the phial.**)

Make your decision, child.

SAM	I need to think. I must think.

(**He starts to move off. ZETA is about to follow.**)

THE DANCER	Zeta!

(**The acolytes surround her.**)

Your soul is mine till the child decides.

ZETA   Remember that, Kirk!

(SAM **exits. Blackout.**)

BACKSTAGE AT THE STADIUM

(**Lights up on** SAM **sitting at the stadium just before the concert that evening. He is holding his guitar. The phial is in his pocket. There are crowd noises offstage – just loud enough for us to be aware that there is a concert audience waiting.** STIG **is onstage next to Sam.**)

STIG   Only a couple of minutes now, eh? Are you nervous?

SAM   I don't know.

STIG   Of course not. I expect someone as great as you doesn't get nerves. You're going to go onstage and *(Imitates some guitar-playing in a rather demented fashion)* . . . except you'll be better than that. And then we'll all be free. Yeeah!

SAM   I hope so.

STIG   Course we will.

(JENNY **comes onstage.**)

Where've you been? Mr Howell was mad when he heard you'd left Kirk.

JENNY *(To Sam)* Are you all right? I've been so worried about you.

SAM   I'm fine.

JENNY Did you find out . . .

SAM   *(Taking out phial)* Yes. I know how to be the Soul-saver now.

JENNY *(Horrified)* Who gave you that?

SAM   The Dancer. It'll make me play brilliantly.

JENNY He's a liar!

SAM	He was a Soul-saver himself.
JENNY	He never saved anyone. He was a great dancer until he took the moonstone. Now he's lost his greatness.
SAM	I must take it. It's my only chance.
JENNY	Don't touch it.
VINCE	*(Entering)* Let the kid take it. If that's what he needs to make the concert work, then take it.
JENNY	It'll destroy him.
VINCE	They want you onstage, kid. If you don't save us, I'll destroy you.

(The crowd can be heard chanting 'Kirk, Kirk, Kirk' softly in the background. This builds and builds during the following section.)

SAM	*(Getting up and picking up guitar)* I'm going on.
JENNY	Tell them the truth, Kirk.
VINCE	Make sure you save us, Kirk.

(SAM climbs onto the raised part of the stage, the lights picking him out alone. The crowd come onstage and surround the raised platform, chanting all the time. Out of the darkness come the following voices.)

THE DANCER	Your soul against all the souls in Limbo.
ZETA	You owe it to us!
JENNY	It'll destroy you!
VINCE	I'll destroy you.

(The crowd chant gets louder as SAM looks at the phial, trying to decide. He thrusts the phial away.)

SAM	*(Desperately)* I'm not Kirk! I'm not Kirk! . . . I'm *(The crowd moves offstage)* . . . I'm . . . What's my name? What's my name? What's my name?

(The spotlight on SAM fades. In the blackout we hear voices.)

MR FURNISS	Sam. Sam.
MRS FURNISS	For God's sake, open your eyes, Sam.
MR FURNISS	Sssh! Look!
MRS FURNISS	His eyelids. Did they move?

THE BEDROOM

(The lights come up slowly, revealing MR and MRS FURNISS kneeling over SAM.)

MR FURNISS	Come on.
MRS FURNISS	Come on, Sam.

(Very slowly SAM lifts his head up from the floor. MRS FURNISS hugs him. MR FURNISS hugs both of them.)

MR FURNISS	Steady.
MRS FURNISS	There'll be a doctor here in a minute, love.
MR FURNISS	Do you feel OK, Sam?
SAM	Sam. That's what I'm called.
MR FURNISS	Eh?
MRS FURNISS	He's muddled.
SAM	It's alright. I was called something else for a while, that's all.
MRS FURNISS	The doctor had best check him for concussion.
SAM	I don't need a doctor. I didn't swallow the moonstone.
MR FURNISS	What's he talking about?
MRS FURNISS	You got a shock from your guitar, Sam. That's what's happened.
MR FURNISS	I'd just got back. Your mum's disconnected it.
SAM	*(Still a bit dreamy)* I'm going to learn to play. Properly. I don't just want to be a star.

MR FURNISS	*(Holding up guitar)* You're not learning on this piece of junk.
MRS FURNISS	Derek!
SAM	I'm going to learn.
MR FURNISS	Aye. Maybe you will.

THE PLAYGROUND AFTER SCHOOL

(DARRYL is doing an idiot dance in front of his large cassette recorder. LISA is painting her nails. KAREN is chewing gum. SAM enters. Darryl snatches up his recorder and tries to make himself inconspicuous.)

LISA	Hiya!
SAM	Hiya!

(SAM is going to walk past them.)

LISA	You're going the wrong way.
KAREN	School's over. Home's that way.
SAM	I'm not going home yet.
KAREN	Are you in trouble with Jackson again?

(SAM shrugs his shoulders.)

LISA	Don't let him keep you too long.
KAREN	You've got to get to the Youthie early, remember? It's talent night.
SAM	Oh that? . . . I'm not going in for it now.
KAREN	Why not?
SAM	*(Laughs)* I haven't got enough talent . . . yet.
LISA	Well come and watch us. We're doing a pop group.
KAREN	We're going to be brilliant.
SAM	I didn't know you'd been practising.

LISA	We haven't.
KAREN	You don't need to when you're brilliant.
SAM	Well, good luck.
LISA	Thanks, but we don't need it.
KAREN	We're going to be . . . just brilliant.

(SAM **exits.** LISA, KAREN **and** DARRYL **watch him go off, then shrug their shoulders at each other.**)

A CLASSROOM

(SAM **is sitting, strumming a guitar.** MR JACKSON **is sitting watching him.**)

MR JACKSON	Now try to go from G to D7, Sam. *(Sam tries and fails)* Try again. *(Sam succeeds)* That's better.
SAM	*(He stops for a moment)* This is hard, isn't it, sir?
MR JACKSON	It's going to get a lot harder yet.
SAM	Do you think I'll ever get the hang of it, sir?
MR JACKSON	How much do you want to succeed?

(SAM **thinks for a moment. He starts strumming again. Blackout.**)

The End

THE MAKING OF THE PLAY

When I was young, I remember being told about Limbo at church. Apparently, when you died you could go to one of three places: Heaven if you'd been very good, Hell if you'd been very bad, and Limbo if you'd been neither one nor the other. People in Limbo just waited and waited until it was decided what to do with them. It was like a dentist's waiting room for the dead. It didn't sound a very exciting place.

I thought about it again, years later, when I read that John Lennon had been killed. The newspaper said – in the neat but meaningless way newspapers like to put things – that he was now up in Rock 'n' Roll Heaven. It made being dead seem quite glamorous, which I thought was strange, because most pop or film stars who have died young have had messy, painful and very undignified deaths.

It set me wondering about all those people who find the pop music industry very exciting and attractive but who never become as successful as the John Lennons. What happens to them when they die? They can't go to Rock 'n' Roll Heaven – they weren't good enough. I suppose they'd have to go to a Rock 'n' Roll Limbo and wait . . . and wait . . . and wait . . .

FOLLOW-UP ACTIVITIES

Group discussion

King of Limbo is a play with a moral in its telling. We might be able to find a couple of moral points in the play and we wouldn't necessarily agree as to what was most important. For instance, for the writer, Adrian Flynn, it seems important that what Sam learns from his time in Limbo, after the shock from the electric guitar, is that success comes from work. Sam, in the final scene, is to be discovered learning basic chords on his guitar from Mr Jackson. You may think there are more important issues. For example, there is also a question about pretence and honesty. Sam's experience in Limbo is uncomfortable because he lies about who he is. He doesn't make up the lie, in the first place, but he becomes quite happy to go along with it until there is a risk of being found out.

- In a small group, consider the moral points made in the play. One is about work being part of success. Another is about honesty being important. What other issues about human relationships and behaviours are brought up? Do you agree with one another about the importance of such issues? If not, what are the differences between you? What do you think the strongest point is that the play makes?

    It may be worth asking someone in the group to make short notes and to report back to the class as a whole after the discussion. Do the other groups see things the same way as you do?

At the beginning of the play, Mr Jackson and Sam have a brief discussion about Sam's behaviour in class and what he expects of his future. During this discussion they exchange the following statements:

MR JACKSON   So you can't read or write music?

    SAM   I don't need to. I'm not trying to be Beethoven, sir. I want to be a rock star.

- Again in a small group, discuss how right you think Sam is in saying this. What does he mean by saying that he's not trying to be Beethoven? Do you think that pop or rock stars need different talents from other musicians? If they do, what are those differences? Do you think that some forms of music are better than others? More enjoyable than others? More serious than others? Try not to simply say 'I like classical more than jazz, or pop more than blues' but explain what it is that is more appealing, more serious for you or offers more challenge. Maybe you play an instrument yourself or are just a keen listener. The difference doesn't matter. There are no rights or wrongs in this debate. What is more interesting is to discover what and why things matter to you and how the experience of music is different or similar for other people.

Often when we talk or read about pop music, we make judgements that seem to have a sense of objective or certain truth about them. Pop music is often supposed to be less important or of a poorer quality than other musical forms. The same is said of different forms of books and art. Yet history has shown that many so-called popular forms become accepted in the mainstream of our cultural lives and may even become considered classics. This has happened to plays by Shakespeare, books by Charles Dickens and songs by the Beatles to name but a very, very few. The criticism that is offered of popular forms of music, books, plays, films, TV and so on is often subjective or personal and not really related to the thing itself at all.

- As a class, discuss the words listed below and how you have experienced them when they have been used to describe the things that you watch, wear, listen, see or do. How do the words work and what is the prejudice that is often carried in their use?

Rare	Distinguished	Chosen	Unique
Exclusive	Irreplaceable	Different	High
Original	Brilliant	Refined	Fine
Ordinary	Average	Usual	Trivial
Dull	Coarse	Crude	Low
Common	Vulgar	Popular	Mass[1]

On page 42 Mr Jackson replies to Sam, who wonders whether he will ever master the playing of a guitar:

MR JACKSON   How much do you want to succeed?

---

1. Taken from Pierre Bourdieu, *Distinction: a social critique of class taste* (Routledge, 1989).

Success is a strange concept because it means different things to different people in different places. Whether you are 'successful' or not also has to do with what you expect of yourself and what other people expect of you. Before starting the discussion suggested below, take a quiet five minutes to write down all the words that you think could describe feelings associated with success and failure. Your teacher could then draw columns on the board and as a class you could put together a list of words connected with success and failure.

- As a whole class, discuss the words in the columns that you have drawn up. Do any words appear in both columns? Are there words in either column that you disagree with and why? Do boys and girls agree or disagree about what success or failure is? Get your teacher to contribute, as well. What is her or his opinion of what is success? Remember that she or he isn't necessarily right. In discussion we are talking about *opinions* and not about undeniable facts. Do you think that if Sam achieves his ambition to be a rock star that he will be a 'success'?

Project

King of Limbo explores the idea of personal images. In this play the images that are offered or possible are those of rock and pop stars and the music industry.

We all have an image. To some extent we may be aware of it and set out to achieve the look that we want. We do this by following fashions and either choosing a particular look or reacting against it in some way. Sometimes we justify this as a way of being 'individual' – different from the 'mass' (of other people). Of course, we are never truly unique or individual because ideas are always borrowed and reworked from somewhere else.

There are also rules which govern what we wear and how we are supposed to behave. If you are at a school with a uniform, then it is very difficult to change altogether the clothing that you wear. You may be able to cheat on small details, but if it goes too far and changes the whole image of the uniform, someone is likely to take you aside and tell you to comply with the rules. In different workplaces there are often rules about what you wear to comply with safety or hygiene regulations. Where there are no official rules, there are often practices which we feel compelled to follow. If you work in a smart office you are unlikely to appear in a boiler suit.

Even in our own time when we can decide for ourselves what clothes we prefer, there are controls on what we wear. In Western cultures, although many women have adopted trousers, jeans or slacks as part of their wardrobe, men have not moved to wearing skirts or dresses. There is no reason at all why this shouldn't happen except for social conformity. You might like to think about this and suggest why it hasn't happened.

In the music industry, the fashions serve quite a different purpose. They are a way of identifying difference from other people or identifying with a style of music. For example, you may like to identify what the following personal images suggest of music styles:

> black leather, studs, long hair, T-shirts
> Doc Martins, torn jeans, wrist bands, T-shirts
> fringed suede jackets, low-cut dresses, plaid shirts, cowboy boots, tight jeans with heavy leather belts
> evening dress suits and formal long skirted dresses
> matching blouses/shirts and smart skirts/trousers

Each item we wear gives messages about where we come from, what we do and contributes to a sense of who we are. They are *signs*. The science of signs is called *semiology*. Each sign, say a leather jacket, gives a number of messages. These messages are called *semic codes*. What messages does a leather jacket give you? What are its semic codes?

You might like to make a list. Not everyone will agree what the semic codes are because they depend on the person doing the seeing and what their past experience is of the object being examined.

Here are some starter suggestions:

rugged	tough	hard
durable	lasting	expensive
cool	distant	impenetrable

During the play, one of the characters (Lisa) imagines that images and style come from nowhere. She says:

LISA   Does he think Madonna had to be taught how to be Madonna?

Of course, we learn things from other people and are not necessarily 'taught' by a teacher. We learn by watching, copying, experimenting. With these thoughts in mind, you might like to put together a project on images of a public figure.

- Identify a single person in the public eye and who interests you enough to collect as much material as you can about them. Photographs from papers and fan magazines are a useful way of building a full picture of the person. What image do you think they are trying to create? What are the semic codes that help build this image? Has the person's image changed at all over time and in what ways? If, for example, you have chosen Madonna, it might be interesting to examine the way in which she has modified or added to her image. Are there any photographs available of her where she is not dressed for the public eye? Who are the people who appear to be an influence on her? Is Marilyn Monroe one of them? What has she taken from such people and how has she used styles and looks for her own image?

  You might like to paste up a huge collage of images of your person alongside all the different people who contribute or borrow from the same 'look'. You may wish to present each image like a portrait gallery. However, it's important that you offer notes and thoughts in written form of what the image is, how the image works, where the image comes from, how the image is adopted and changed. The reader needs to understand from your work the semiology of this individual. Don't simply offer a biography or a fan account to read.

Written work

ZETA   Today we're going to make that big jump between terminals. Kirk Klein, the Soul-saver, is going to throw the switch that sends us surging through the ether. There'll be no resistance. We're not going to be ampered; we're finally going ohm. So let's switch onto

standby for a while to recharge. This is Zeta
Morita, your electric preacher telling all you
live-wires to be here again this afternoon,
when we'll plug back into the cosmic mains.

The speech above from page 23 uses electrical puns (a play on
words) to liven the language and give it a 'charge'. And that's
another pun on electricity! Some people do this as a habit
because they enjoy the way that language and speech works.
How many can you identify in Zeta's speech? The first one is
'jump' as in the jump leads for starting a car from another car's
battery.

- Write your own speech for Zeta using puns. You may like to
  continue with the electrical theme or 'switch' to another theme and
  associated words such as:

    Baking: bread, dough, crumbs, cake, biscuit, rise, knead,
    yeast, cook, bake, stir, glaze, icing, rub-in, creaming,
    rolling-out, cutting, fill, beating.

    Horses: bridle, bit, saddle, tail, rein, gallop, canter, charge,
    cavalry, ride, trot, snaffle, hock, wither, hoof, shoe, mane,
    braid, brush, curry, crop, harness.

  You may like to make up your own category. To help you find
  words it may be useful to use a thesaurus, which lists words in
  related families.

In the section The Making of the Play, Adrian Flynn makes a
comment about the way in which newspapers write about the
lives and deaths of public people. It may be interesting to collect
all the papers from one day's publication and look at the
different manner in which each paper treats a particular public
person that has made the news. Are there photographs which
suppport the story? Is the photograph sympathetic? How does
the reporter talk about the person? Is the reporter
complimentary or negative about him/her?

- Imagine that you are the reporter asked to write about Kirk Klein.
  Choose one of the papers below and write in the style that you
  might expect to read in its pages:

> *The Daily Telegraph*
> *The Times*
> *The Guardian*
> *The Sun*
> *The Sunday Sport*
> Your local paper.
> It may be interesting to collect together all the reports in the class and compare the stories and see if you agree with the style of writing for particular papers.

After the electric shock from the amplifier, Sam finds himself in Limbo. This is a state that the playwright, in the section The Making of the Play, has described as being between Heaven and Hell. It's also the way we describe a state of being that is neither here nor there – a moving-on from something in the past, but not yet achieving what we expect or want of the future. For example, for some people there is a period between leaving school and their first job or taking a place at college which they might think of as being in Limbo.

- Imagine that you, like Sam, have travelled to a Limbo of your own. However, unlike Sam, who has gone to a musical Limbo, you have gone to a Limbo which is connected to your own life, hobby or interest. It could, for instance, be connected with horses or baking, motorbikes or fashion. What is this Limbo like and who are the people that inhabit the place? Write your own imaginative story.

Design

Every play involves creating an imaginary world when it becomes a production upon the stage, just as it becomes an imaginary world when we read it from the page. This creating of an imaginary world takes many forms and many talents. Below are three projects that you may consider doing.

- Design the costume and make-up for Kirk Klein's concert. What sort of musician is he and what sort of image does he want to project? You might like to collect photo-images of other rock stars that you think are similar. If you have a stage make-up box you might like to try creating the image you have in mind on a friend. Remember to make sure that your friend has no allergies to make-up!

Draw sketches or use photo-montages to show us how this person may look in their costume. What are the colours and fabrics that you might use?

- The Ever-readies are a group of fans. They take their name, of course, from batteries. Design costumes for these people. It might help to get a battery and study it and see in what way you can adapt the clothing to mimic or suggest the shapes and colours. Draw sketches and make notes of colours, fabrics, etc.
- An important prop (or stage object) in the play is the phial of the moonstone. This has magical properties and is very important in the story. Since it has no description at all, you have the opportunity of designing something from your imagination. It needs to be large enough and imposing enough to attract the attention of an audience. It may be, for example, that you have electrical skills and could make up a model that glows. (But if you do, be sure to use batteries *not* mains electricity for reasons of safety.) Start with sketch plans showing its outward appearance and how it may be constructed. If you have time and the resources, you may like to make the phial.

Drama ideas

Drama is a very good way of exploring a script, particularly if you are going to mount a production of the play. It is a way of organising your thinking and trying ways of showing things – making live theatre from a script. The best drama ideas usually come from you, as you will know what interests you about the play and what needs to be worked on. The following are only ideas to start you off. Think about other possibilities and follow those up too!

- Kirk Klein has been invited to a press conference. Take roles of reporters from different papers and magazines and ask the questions of someone in the role of Kirk Klein. What angle does your publication take? How does it interpret the legend of Kirk Klein? How does Kirk Klein project himself?
- As a practical movement exercise, imagine that you are the battery of believers and make up the 'dance of passing electrical current back and forth'. How does electricity move and how do you show that in your body movements?
- Explore the idea of arriving in Limbo. This needs some preparation.

Agree a drama lesson in which you might carry this out. You will need to bring in as much old newspaper as you can comfortably carry and a large roll of sticky tape. Choose a piece of music that you think fits the idea of moving from reality to unreality.

On the day of the exercise you will need to split the group into pairs – one person to be wrapped in the newspaper and the other to do the wrapping. It will help if the studio or the room is as dark as possible. Make a large mat of newspaper with the edges overlapping and taped so that you can lie comfortably with your knees and arms tucked close to you. Get a partner to finish the wrapping so that you are entirely enclosed in a paper egg.

The mood needs to be very still and quiet. When everyone is wrapped, the partners need to withdraw to the side of the room and the music begun. Slowly explore your feelings about this egg-like world and think about being born into Limbo land. What are you tempted to do and why? As you are born into Limbo, what is it that you see? Imagine that all this is new and that the other paper eggs are moving into Limbo too.

If you have a video camera available, it may be useful to record the experience so that you can talk about it afterwards. The partners will have valuable observations to make, too, about what the scene looks like from the outside.

The mood of the exercise can be changed considerably by using coloured lighting and different forms and volumes of music.